See This Christ

Linda Lysakowski

Copyright © 2020 Linda Lysakowski

No portions of this publication may be reproduced, distributed, transmitted, stored, performed, displayed, adapted, or used in any form or manner without prior written permission, except for certain limited noncommercial uses permitted by the United States Copyright Act, such as brief quotations embodied in critical reviews.

ISBN: 978-1-7347992-0-0

Dedication

For late husband, Marty, who was always ***The Face of Jesus*** for me, and for my spiritual director, Steve, who has continually helped me ***See This Christ*** in new and ever-changing ways.

Acknowledgements

I wish to thank my dear friends for giving me insights, suggestions, and encouragement during the writing of this book—especially Father Ron Zanoni, whose insightful homilies continue to inspire me and influence my spirituality; Sister Janet Ackerman OP, whose strength and spirituality unceasingly encourage me; Father Tony Hughes, whose spirituality and sense of humor are always uplifting; and Stephen Nill, JD, editor, publisher, coach, and friend, who has helped me become a better writer.

About the Cover

The elevation of the Body and Blood of Christ is a meaningful moment in the Catholic Mass. The tradition began in the middle ages, as part of the Franco-Roman Mass. People during this time had started to move away from receiving the Eucharist at every Mass, but they still wanted to "See This Christ" revealed to the people. It has special meaning for me because, like many Catholics, I was away from the sacraments for several years. One day during the Mass, when the priest elevated the Body and Blood, I was overcome by a voice telling me I needed to return to Jesus and receive him fully. That moment was the inspiration for my original poem, which this book is based on, so it naturally become a moment I wanted to capture on the cover of the book.

Preface

If you've read my earlier book, **The Face of Jesus,** this is sort of a sequel to it, although the title is different. This book is based on a poem I wrote more than forty years ago. I was really sick with an upper respiratory infection one Easter and could not make any of the services of the Triduum. My dearest late husband, Marty, who was an excellent cook, made a wonderful meatloaf on the first day I felt like eating and it gave me the strength to write this poem. After forty years, I finally decided to turn it into a book and, as with **The Face of Jesus,** an accompanying study guide. I hope this book will help you **See This Christ** as I see him—a loving, forgiving God; a wise teacher; a compassionate healer; and a joy-filled friend. As they say, "Seeing is believing!"

See This Christ

*See this Christ who is laughing,
and dancing with the children in the streets.*

*See this Christ who is teaching,
and longing for all people to be free.*

*See this Christ who is angry
at the way we have denied our Creator's love.*

*See this Christ who is touching,
healing broken bodies, broken souls.*

*See this Christ who kneels before you
washing feet of sinful people.*

*See this Christ who hangs here bleeding,
weeping, dying for your sins.*

*See this Christ in all His glory,
risen now triumphantly.*

*See this Christ who loves you,
and wants you to be with Him every day.
Yes, he wants you to be with Him in all ways.
Every day.*

Table of Contents

Chapter One: The Laughing Christ   1

Chapter Two: The Teaching Christ   7

Chapter Three: The Angry Christ   15

Chapter Four: The Healing Christ   21

Chapter Five: The Servant Christ   31

Chapter Six: The Dying Christ   37

Chapter Seven: The Risen Christ   43

Chapter Eight: The Loving Christ   49

Chapter One: The Laughing Christ

See this Christ who is laughing,
and dancing with the children in the streets.

Although there is no scripture passage saying "Jesus laughed," as there is, "Jesus wept," if you study scriptures you will come to the conclusion that Jesus was a joyful person and there are many scripture passages that express his joyfulness, celebrating with his friends. In fact, he was even accused of perhaps being *too* joyful.

See This Christ

> **Luke 7:34 (NIV)** *The Son of Man came eating and drinking, and you say, 'Here is a glutton and a drunkard, a friend of tax collectors and sinners.'*

While Mark doesn't specifically mention Jesus laughing, he shows his love for children in 10:16 (NIV):

> *And he took the children in his arms, placed his hands on them and blessed them.*

It is hard to imagine Jesus taking children into his arms and blessing them without picturing the children and Jesus laughing together. Children are naturally drawn to happy people, and I have to believe so many children flocked to Jesus because of his laughing, joyful nature.

Jesus' first miracle was at the wedding feast at Cana. What happier time is there than a wedding reception where families laugh and dance together, and drink wine together. Again, we find this an occasion where it is almost certain Jesus laughed and danced. Later, in Matthew 9:15 (NIV), he tells his disciples it is not a time to mourn but rather be joyful and enjoy his presence.

> *Jesus answered, "How can the guests of the bridegroom mourn while he is with them? The time will come when the bridegroom will be taken from them; then they will fast.*

We need to enjoy Jesus' joyfulness within us, and to see his joy in others.

Jesus, of course, was fully human and fully divine so just as joy and laughter are a part of human life, along with sadness and tears, they most certainly were a part of his life as well.

Chapter One: The Laughing Christ

Is there a human being alive who has never laughed? Even when we face illness and calamity, there is laughter. It is part of human nature. I know I've witnessed people knowing they have hours, days, or weeks to live, and yet their sense of humor remains. It was one of the things I loved most about my husband, Marty—even when his time on earth was coming to an end, he laughed and joked with family, friends, nursing staff, and visitors. In fact, one of his great joys was a joke book my son-in-law brought him in the nursing home and he would tell jokes (many times potty humor) to the nurses and make their day brighter. He was a real "epiphany" to all those around him because of his joyfulness. A wise priest coined a new word by making epiphany a verb, so as he would say, Marty "epiphanized" his caretakers. And, isn't that what we're all called by Christ to do, "epiphanize" our world, so matter how small or large that world might be. Sometimes laughter might be the best way to "epiphanize."

And I have a friend who, after having a total colostomy, even as the surgeon was marking her shoulder for the surgery that would put the port into her for weekly chemotherapy, showed her usual quick wit. She shouted at the surgeon as he started marking her right shoulder, "You can't put it there!" Taken aback, he asked why. "It will interfere with my golf swing!" was her reply.

And another friend who, while he was experiencing great turmoil in his life, always found a way to cheer me with his sense of humor, recalling good times we had together.

It must be truly sad to lose your sense of humor.

Jesus used Semitic irony and humor a lot in his teaching. I have to believe that humor is part of God's nature. How many times have you been reminded of God's sense of humor? It has been said that humans make plans, and God laughs at those plans because God has other plans for us.

If you doubt that God has a sense of humor, sometimes we need to look at nature to see its evidence. Just watch animals interact. While they may not have human intelligence, it's obvious that they are blessed with a sense of humor. Have you ever watched monkeys at the zoo? They always seem to attract the biggest crowd because of their antics. Perhaps we see ourselves in their shenanigans. I sometimes think God's creation might be laughing at us humans and wonder if we belong inside or outside the cages at the zoo. And I am convinced that God looks down on us and surely must be laughing at our foolish antics, but also laughs and dances with us when are filled with joy.

To imagine Jesus not laughing and enjoying life is a denial of his humanity. He said in the Beatitudes, as recorded in Matthew and Luke.

> **Luke 6:21 (NAS)** *Blessed are you who weep now, for you shall laugh.*

I believe Jesus intended us to laugh, be joyful, and to share our sense of humor with others, to share the joy of Jesus with them.

And, who better to laugh with than children?

Perhaps one of the passages that points this out clearly is Mark 10: 13-14, 16 (NIV):

> *People were bringing little children to Jesus for him to place his hands on them, but the disciples rebuked them. When Jesus saw this, he was indignant. He said to them, "Let the children come to me and do not hinder them, for*

Chapter One: The Laughing Christ

the reign of God belongs to such as these"…..and he took the children in his arms, placed his hands on them and blessed them.

His indignance is indicative of the angry Christ we'll meet in a future chapter. But his joy was evident with the children. Jesus welcomed the little children and indeed told us that we are to receive God with a childlike innocence in order to enter the reign of God. Jesus asks us to have childlike faith. While semantics professors might argue the differences between childlike and childish, the accepted definitions, while basically the same, are commonly accepted as having different connotations. To be childish is generally meant to be pejorative—it implies petulance, immaturity, narcissism; whereas being childlike implies innocence and honesty.

I think we have all seen adults who act childish, who demand that things be done their way, who throw tantrums (maybe they don't lie down on the floor in the supermarket and kick their feet, but they throw an adult tantrum—if I don't get my way, I'm taking my marbles and going home). Being childish once you reach adulthood is not an endearing quality, is it? We've all probably acted childishly at times ourselves. I suspect most of us have at one time or another sulked when things didn't go our way.

But Jesus praised those who were *childlike*—who are honest in expressing their feelings, who have a form of innocence that is not being naïve and expecting everything to be sunshine and roses, but who try to see the best in others. While sometimes even his own disciples fell short in this regard, he loved them anyway, so don't

See This Christ

despair if you fall short sometimes too. I think Jesus values us and is with us most when we are joyful. Don't be afraid to laugh and dance with Jesus with the innocence of a child.

Chapter Two: The Teaching Christ

*See this Christ who is teaching,
and longing for all people to be free.*

There are far more scripture passages about the teachings of Jesus than there are of Jesus being joyful and laughing. All four gospels focus on the teachings of Jesus. What does he teach about? God's love for humankind, the reign of God, loving our neighbors as ourselves, ethics and morality, and more. How did he teach? Mostly through parables, which he expanded on with his disciples, sharing with them the meaning of his parables.

See This Christ

Parables are an interesting choice. Why did using stories (parables) consume so much of Jesus' teaching?

I find it interesting that in both the 21st century business world, and in the world of nonprofits, which I've worked in for more than thirty years, suddenly storytelling has become a hot buzzword. You can attend conferences just on storytelling for nonprofits. You can take courses in storytelling. You can hire consultants to help you tell your organization's story to donors or customers. Maybe Jesus was way ahead of his time! I think the reason storytelling has become so popular in the nonprofit and business worlds the past few years, is because people are starting to realize that the best way to get across their point is to put a human face on their story. In the nonprofit world this means making your case for support, why should people donate to your nonprofit. It's not because you need money, need a new building, or hire more staff, it's because they want to help the people you serve—they want to change lives and save lives. In the business world, it's not selling the features on your product, it's selling the benefits of it—in other words, "sell the sizzle, not the steak."

Jesus did this through parables. He asked us to put ourselves in the position of the people, or sometimes the objects, in his stories.

Think about the parable of the Prodigal Son, for example. When we read this story in Luke 15, we tend to identify with one of the characters. At times, we might identify with the father—worrying, watching every day for his son to return home. At other times we may identify with the prodigal son—seeing that our choices were the wrong ones and wanting to come home and seek forgiveness. At other times, we may identify with the brother who resented being a steadfast support for his father

Chapter Two: The Teaching Christ

and now seeing his father welcoming the son who was not there when his father needed him. Jesus could easily have just said—be patient and good things will come, repent of your sins, and don't resent those whom God loves even if they haven't made good choices. But this story shows us real human beings who struggled with the same things we struggle with and how they overcame their struggles.

Similarly, in the parable of the Good Samaritan (Matthew 5:43-48), Jesus again uses his gift of storytelling to tell us how important compassion is and that we should love or neighbor as ourselves. Again, this story finds us identifying with different characters at different times in our life. Sometimes we may feel like the man who was beaten and robbed, left to die alone in a ditch by the side of the road. Perhaps we haven't literally been beaten up, but we feel we've suffered wrong at the hands of someone—a stranger, friend, a family member. We feel emotionally beaten down and hopeless because we are alone in our suffering and perhaps feel no one cares enough to help us. At other times we may feel like the priest or the Pharisee; perhaps we pass by others in need because we are busy with our lives and don't want to get involved with other people's troubles. We may even feel like those in need deserve their situation—if they would get a job, they wouldn't be homeless; if they didn't drink or gamble, they'd have money to buy food; if they had planned better, they wouldn't be out of a job; if they'd taken better care of their health, they wouldn't be bankrupt because of their healthcare costs. If they hadn't traveled to take refuge for themselves and their families in a strange land, they wouldn't be separated from family members, treated like criminals, or deported. And sometimes we feel like the good Samaritan who showed compassion and gave without expectation of being repaid.

Once again, Jesus could have just said love your neighbor, and everyone is your neighbor—even the priest and the Pharisee who ignored the suffering of a stranger—but he told us a story so we could see that these situations happen in everyone's life and his teaching about loving all God's creation has meaning today just as it did then.

Sometimes, his parables spoke more in terms of things, not people, such as in the parable of the mustard seed (Matthew 13: 31-32) and the parable of the good and bad soil (Matthew 13 1-8). We sometimes can relate our lives to nature as well. The mustard seed, the smallest of seeds, becomes a large bush and a haven for the birds to take shelter. Even if we think we are insignificant, we can do great things. And we can identify with the different types of soil—sometimes our lives may be rocky, sometimes we feel the "weeds" are choking us, sometimes the wind scatters us in too many directions, and yet, if we are open to God's word, if it is planted it good soil (an open mind) it flourishes. We may even wonder why a farmer would waste good seed throwing it about willy-nilly to land on rocks and thorns where it will surely not flourish. But this parable tells us a lot about God's love—it is offered freely to all, even those who may reject it. And sometimes it even clings where we don't expect it. I know I've often marveled at plants growing out of the cracks in huge boulders, or mountains and wondered where they get the nourishment to survive. And,

Chapter Two: The Teaching Christ

living in the desert, I've been amazed at the amount of flora and fauna that can live in such a barren environment. My favorite trees, the Bristlecone Pine trees, survive at the very top of the tree line in very alkaline soil, and yet are the oldest living things on earth. This parable might prove God's love can break through even the harshest denial of that love and survive in impossible situations. It is never for us to say who has felt the penetration of God's love, even if it appears to be swept away by the wind or unable to penetrate a hardened heart.

Jesus used parables things that the people of his time understood—farming, fishing, and so on—so his stories would be relatable to his audience. But they are just as relevant to us today when we understand the deeper meaning of the story.

It is interesting that most of the time when he taught using parables, later as he was alone with his disciples, he elaborated more on the story and revealed the meaning. Was it because his disciples were dense and didn't understand his message? Or because he wanted them to develop their own stories that could then relate the truths he preached in a way that would be understandable to their various audiences? Saint Paul certainly told stories in his letters that related to his different audiences.

Sometimes Jesus taught more directly and not in parables. The most evident of these instances was the Beatitudes.

He was pretty direct in the sermon on the mount (Matthew 5: 3-10) or the sermon on the plain (Luke 6:20-49).

> **Matthew 5:3-10 (NIRV)** *Blessed are those who are spiritually needy. The reign of God belongs to them.*
> *Blessed are those who are sad. They will be comforted.*

See This Christ

Blessed are those who are free of pride. They will be given the earth.

Blessed are those who are hungry and thirsty for what is right. They will be filled.

Blessed are those who show mercy. They will be shown mercy.

Blessed are those who are pure of heart. They will see God.

Blessed are those who make peace. They will be called sons and daughters of God.

Blessed are those who suffer for doing what is right. The reign of God belongs to them.

He is pretty clear about what God asks of us—to feel the stirrings of the Holy Spirit and respond to them, to weep for injustice, to walk humbly with God, to seek the right path, to show mercy, to not harbor hatred in our hearts, to turn our swords into plowshares, and to be bold enough to stand up for what is right even if it is unpopular.

This is what God asks of us.

The other time Jesus was very direct about what God expects of us is when he was asked, which of the commandments was the greatest. He answered with two admonitions.

(Mark 12:28-31 NIRV) *Love God with all your heart, all your mind, all your soul, all your strength. And love your neighbor as yourself.*

I truly believe that when we meet God face to face, we will be asked three questions (not that God needs the

Chapter Two: The Teaching Christ

answers—because our hearts are known to God, but rather, because we need to answer these questions for ourselves). Those questions will be:

- Did you love me with all your heart, mind, soul, and strength?
- Did you love your neighbor as yourself?
- If the answers to those two questions are, "yes," how did you put that love into action?

Loving God typically comes easy for many of us, although sometimes we question God—why does a little child get cancer and die? Why do we have war? Why does God let us, or our loved ones, suffer? But loving God with all your heart means trusting! And that isn't always so easy!

Loving our neighbor is even harder. Who is our neighbor? Everyone. The Muslim, the Jew, the Atheist, the Satanist, as well as the Christian. The gay, lesbian, transgender, bisexual, as well as the straight person. The African American, the Latino, the Indigenous person, as well as the Anglo Saxon. The progressive as well as the conservative. The criminal as well as the victim. And, don't forget, it starts with loving ourselves. That doesn't mean narcissism or thinking we are always right; it means we strive to be a person who deserves to be loved, even though God loves us whether we are deserving or not. A dear friend once told me that humility is really another word for Truth. We don't have to be self-deprecating to be humble. We need to accept the truth about ourselves—the good and the bad—in order to love ourselves.

There are so many scripture passages relating the wisdom of Christ the teacher, that I could fill an entire book on this aspect

See This Christ

of Christ. Even religions that do not recognize Jesus as the son of God, see him as a great prophet. His teachings, while sometimes in the form of admonitions, were predominately those of a loving, forgiving God who calls us to be the same. He told his followers that he did not come to abolish the law, but to fulfill it. If we follow his teachings to love God, and to love our neighbor, we are set free from the pain and suffering of the world, while still living and acting the world as Christ the teacher calls us to do.

Chapter Three: The Angry Christ

See this Christ who is angry
at the way we have denied our Creator's love.

The most common image we have of the angry Christ was when he drove the money lenders and merchants out of the temple. However, there were other moments in scripture where we see Jesus, at the very least, perturbed at the folly of humankind. Perhaps even angry, although the scriptures may not use that word.

The first instance where Jesus' anger is mentioned is in Mark.

Mark 3:1-6 (NIRV) *Another time Jesus went into the synagogue, and a man with a shriveled hand was there.*

See This Christ

Some of them were looking for a reason to accuse Jesus, so they watched him closely to see if he would heal him on the Sabbath. Jesus said to the man with the shriveled hand, "Stand up in front of everyone." Then Jesus asked them, "Which is lawful on the Sabbath: to do good or to do evil, to save life or to kill?" But they remained silent. He looked around at them in anger and, deeply distressed at their stubborn hearts, said to the man, "Stretch out your hand." He stretched it out, and his hand was completely restored. Then the Pharisees went out and began to plot with the Herodians how they might kill Jesus.

His anger was the result of seeing how the Pharisees were more concerned with the letter of the law than they were about caring for those who needed healing. We sometimes concern ourselves far more with the letter of the law, and this disappoints and, yes, even angers Jesus. An example of this in modern times is apparent in cities and countries that pass laws making it illegal to give water to the homeless or sanctuary to the refugees. People have actually been prosecuted for making a humane gesture of tenderness and welcome. Is this what Jesus would do? Yes, we need laws in order to be free but there are times when unjust laws must be questioned, and a higher good must be served.

The most prominent image of the angry Jesus is the one both Mark and John tell us about in their Gospels.

Mark 11:15 (NLT) *When they arrived back in Jerusalem, Jesus entered the temple and began to drive out the people buying and selling animals for sacrifices.*

Chapter Three: The Angry Christ

He knocked over the tables of the money changers and the chairs of those selling doves.

John 2:15-17 (NLT) *Jesus made a whip from some ropes and chased them all out of the temple. He drove out the sheep and cattle, scattered the money changers' coins over the floor, and turned over their tables. Then, going over to the people who sold doves, he told them, "Get these things out of here. Stop turning my father's house into a marketplace!" Then his disciples remembered this prophecy from the scriptures: "Passion for God's house will consume me."*

So, is Jesus against capitalism and free enterprise? Not really. He was friends with merchants, tax collectors, prostitutes, and others. What he was really telling his followers, including us, is that prayer is more important than merchandising. He understood that poor people could not afford the cost of doves to sacrifice. He showed us that true prayer comes from the heart. He told us parables of the widow's mite and of the Pharisee and the tax collector praying in the temple. What he really gets angry about is when we fail to give God thanks for our blessings, to ask forgiveness when we need it, and to pray for each other. Not only to pray, in fact, but to put our thoughts and prayers into action. To fight for what is right, just as he did when he overturned the tables in the temple.

Jesus, after all, is fully human as well as fully divine. So, of course he had human feelings, including anger.

He even showed annoyance in a passage that is usually associated more with the happy Jesus—the wedding at Cana.

See This Christ

John 2: 1-5 (NIV) *On the third day a wedding took place at Cana in Galilee. Jesus' mother was there, and Jesus and his disciples had also been invited to the wedding. When the wine was gone, Jesus' mother said to him, "They have no more wine." "Woman, why do you involve me?" Jesus replied. "My hour has not yet come." His mother said to the servants, "Do whatever he tells you."*

While we might not think of Jesus as angry during this scenario, he certainly was annoyed. And annoyance can be a form of anger. He didn't call Mary, "Mother," but rather, *"Woman."* Those of you who are mothers, I think would feel as I would if one of my kids called me, "woman" in that context. We would most likely take it as being disrespectful. Mary didn't really react to this, but rather took the proactive stance of turning to the servants and saying, "Do whatever he tells you." This story tells us something about Jesus and about his mother. Maybe he was feeling a bit tremulous about this whole thing—he had not yet performed any public miracles. What if he failed? It may have been his doubt that made him perturbed, even at his own mother. But she let it go and moved on.

How often does our doubt and fear cause us to be perturbed or even angry? Our anger is most often not justified. We get angry when things don't go our way, when someone insults us, when our fears get the best of us. Jesus didn't get angry at any of this. What angered him was when people denied God's love for humanity. When they held to human-made laws and traditions more than they cared for each other.

Chapter Three: The Angry Christ

Another instance where Jesus gets angry it's because humans tend to be judgmental and unforgiving.

> **John 7:53-55 – 8:11 (NIV)** *One day while Jesus was teaching in the temple courts, Pharisees and teachers of the law brought in a woman who had been caught in the act of adultery. Forcing her to stand before all the people, they asked Jesus: "Teacher, this woman was caught in the act of adultery. In the Law, Moses commanded us to stone such women. Now, what do you say?"*

If Jesus consented to stone the woman, he would have been breaking the Roman law and causing the people to distrust him. However, refusing to stone her could be construed as treating the law of Moses too lightly.

> *Knowing they were trying to catch him in a trap, Jesus bent down and began writing on the ground with his finger. They persisted in questioning him until Jesus stood up and said: "Let any of you who is without sin be the first to throw a stone at her."*
>
> *Then he resumed his bent position to write again on the ground. One by one, from oldest to youngest, the people slipped away quietly until Jesus and the woman were left alone.*
>
> *Straightening up again, Jesus asked, "Woman, where are they? Has no one condemned you?"*
>
> *She replied, "No one, sir."*
>
> *"Then neither do I condemn you," stated Jesus. "Go now and leave your life of sin."*

See This Christ

Jesus was not angry with the sinner, but with the self-righteous who wanted to kill her. This was indeed a people who refused to follow God's mandate to love others, to be forgiving, and not to judge others lest we be judged. While he didn't outwardly display anger, he channeled that anger into wisdom. It is widely held that what Jesus wrote on the ground were the sins of those about to stone the woman. Perhaps greed, cheating, gossiping, denying help to the widow and the orphan, not welcoming the stranger in their land.

We sometimes get angry at the wrong things, but we have every right to be angry at the injustices we see in life. Injustices that surround us every day, but that anger should be channeled into positive action. What can we do about those injustices? Even if it is something very small. Remember that Bethlehem was a small town, but God worked great things there. And God can work great things in us, if we let it happen. If, instead of just being angry, we find positive solutions to those injustices.

What angers Jesus most is when we deny God's love, when we refuse to love God and love our neighbor as ourselves.

Chapter Four: The Healing Christ

See this Christ who is touching,
healing broken bodies, broken souls.

The stories of Christ healing are numerous in scripture. As a woman, I always sort of chuckle when I read the story of Jesus healing Peter's mother-in-law.

See This Christ

Matthew 8:14-15 (NIV) *When Jesus came into Peter's home, He saw his mother-in-law lying sick in bed with a fever. He touched her hand, and the fever left her; and she got up and waited on him.*

Isn't it just like a woman to be healed and then immediately to get up and wait on her family, her friends, and her healer! But I think that's what the healing Jesus is all about. Restoring us, even if from a minor illness so we can be about the work of God in our daily lives. This story also resonates with me because it shows us healing doesn't always have to be dramatic, life-changing event, as it was in some of the other healings Jesus performed. Sometimes it is simple as it was in the story I related in the introduction to this book. I didn't have a life-threatening illness, nor was I at death's door, but a simple upper respiratory infection was devastating for me because it prevented me from going about my daily tasks and even attending church. So, while Jesus didn't come and raise me from my deathbed, he inspired Marty to cook me a meal that was nourishing and brought my body back to its normal state. Sometimes maybe all we should ask of Jesus is the healing that will help us live our lives that allow us to go on serving others.

And, although Jesus performed this healing himself, in our lives he often sends others—doctors, nurses, priests, family members, or friends, to do the work of healing.

Another healing story, a bit more dramatic, is the story of the healing of the Centurion's servant.

Matthew 8: 5-13 (NAS) *And when Jesus entered Capernaum, a centurion came to Him, imploring Him,*

Chapter Four: The Healing Christ

and saying, "Lord, my servant is lying paralyzed at home, fearfully tormented." Jesus said to him, "I will come and heal him." But the centurion said, "Lord, I am not worthy for you to come under my roof, but just say the word, and my servant will be healed." For I also am a man under authority, with soldiers under me; and I say to this one, 'Go!' and he goes, and to another, 'Come!' and he comes, and to my slave, 'Do this!' and he does it." Now when Jesus heard this, he marveled and said to those who were following, "Truly I say to you, I have not found such great faith with anyone in Israel. I say to you that many will come from east and west, and recline at the table with Abraham, Isaac, and Jacob in the kingdom of heaven; but the sons of the kingdom will be cast out into the outer darkness; in that place there will be weeping and gnashing of teeth." And Jesus said to the centurion, "Go; it shall be done for you as you have believed." And the servant was healed that very moment.

This healing story is remarkable for several reasons. First the centurion is a Roman, not a Jew. Second, he is not asking for healing for himself, but for a servant. Surely servants were a dime a dozen, or a denarii a dozen to be more accurate, so why would the centurion show this much concern for a servant? Third, here is a non-Jew who shows the ultimate faith; he is convinced that Jesus can and will, indeed, heal his servant.

A couple of lessons we can learn from this are first not to judge people of other faiths. We know from scripture that the Romans thought the Jews were foolish to expect a Messiah to come save them, and many of the Jews themselves thought the Messiah's purpose was to free them from the occupation of Rome and restore their land to them. However, this centurion came to Jesus and was accepted by him. Most likely he would have expected rejection by this Christ, since most Jews hated the Romans. But Jesus, was *not* most Jews. Repeatedly he told us to accept all people and, repeatedly, he healed Gentile, Jew, and those who perhaps didn't accept any God, or thought they had been forgotten by God. Our lesson from this is that we should never think that Jesus will reject someone's plea because they don't look like us, or they don't worship in the same way we do, or even that they may be our persecutors.

Secondly, the centurion's care for his servant is to be commended. And, like the centurion, interceding for someone who is homeless, poor, or disabled, is our duty. Jesus expects us to show concern for all people, even those may seem insignificant to us. We're back to that "love your neighbor as yourself" theme again. And who is our neighbor? Everyone.

Thirdly, faith is often alive in people from whom we don't expect it. The reason Jesus listened to the centurion's plea is that he was most likely astounded to see this faith coming from a Roman. So, while we need to remember the poor are suffering are our neighbors, we also must remember that the wealthy and powerful are also our neighbor.

Another story of how faith can bring about healing is the story of the woman with the hemorrhage.

> **Mark 5:25-34 (NAS)** *A woman who had had a hemorrhage for twelve years, and had endured much*

Chapter Four: The Healing Christ

at the hands of many physicians, and had spent all that she had and was not helped at all, but rather had grown worse— after hearing about Jesus, she came up in the crowd behind him and touched His cloak. For she thought, "If I just touch his garments, I will get well." Immediately the flow of her blood was dried up; and she felt in her body that she was healed of her affliction. Immediately Jesus, perceiving in himself that the power proceeding from him had gone forth, turned around in the crowd and said, "Who touched my garments?" And his disciples said to him, "You see the crowd pressing in on you, and you say, 'Who touched me?'" And he looked around to see the woman who had done this. But the woman fearing and trembling, aware of what had happened to her, came and fell down before him and told him the whole truth. And he said to her, "Daughter, your faith has made you well; go in peace and be healed of your affliction."

This is another story of instantaneous healing, which isn't always the way God works, but it did happen for this unnamed woman. What is interesting about this story is that she didn't even ask Jesus for help, she merely touched his robe. Most likely she was afraid, after all she was a woman, she had been suffering for years, and perhaps, like the centurion, she wasn't even a Jew, so why would this Christ even take the time to see her face in the crowd, let alone heal her.

It is hard, sometimes, to be brave, to even ask for healing. And sometimes our expectations may be low—if modern medicine hasn't been able to help me, why should I trust this Christ to heal

See This Christ

me? But his love and tenderness are boundless. It is our faith that heals us, sometimes instantly, sometimes over a period of time, and sometimes in ways we don't expect. I know there are times when I feel a great physical weakness and sometimes it goes away gradually; other times it seems something can strengthen me in an instant. Often it is the reception of the Body and Blood of Christ that seems to burst forth filling my body with strength. Other times it is hearing the word of God, or even just hearing a song, that can strengthen me. Even if Christ is not here face-to-face to bring us healing, he sends us healing in many ways, if we just listen, and ask for healing. Learn to touch Jesus' garments in whatever way you can.

Other people in scripture were bolder, they had no hesitation to ask Jesus for healing for themselves, such as Bartimaeus and the ten lepers.

> **Mark 10:46-52 (NRSV)** *They came to Jericho. As he and his disciples and a large crowd were leaving Jericho, a blind beggar, Bartimaeus, son of Timaeus, was sitting by the roadside. When he heard that it was Jesus of Nazareth, he began to shout out and say, "Jesus, Son of David, have mercy on me!" Many sternly ordered him to be quiet, but he cried out even more loudly, "Son of David, have mercy on me!" Jesus stood still and said, "Call him here." And they called the blind man, saying to him, "Take heart; get up, he is calling you." So, throwing off his cloak, he sprang up and came to Jesus. Then Jesus said to him, "What do you want me to do for you?" The blind man said to him, "My teacher, let me see again." Jesus said to him, "Go, your faith has made you well."*

Chapter Four: The Healing Christ

Immediately he regained his sight and followed him on the way.

Like others, Bartimaeus was healed because of his faith. But unlike the woman with the hemorrhage, his friends encouraged him to seek out Jesus. Sometimes we must listen to others to find our way to Christ.

The ten lepers also sought out Jesus.

> **Luke 17-11-19 (NIV)** *Now on his way to Jerusalem, Jesus traveled along the border between Samaria and Galilee. As he was going into a village, ten men who had leprosy met him. They stood at a distance and called out in a loud voice, "Jesus, Master, have pity on us!" When he saw them, he said, "Go, show yourselves to the priests." And as they went, they were cleansed. One of them, when he saw he was healed, came back, praising God in a loud voice. He threw himself at Jesus' feet and thanked him—and he was a Samaritan. Jesus asked, "Were not all ten cleansed? Where are the other nine? Has no one returned to give praise to God except this foreigner?" Then he said to him, "Rise and go; your faith has made you well."*

However, the one difference in this story is that nine of those who were healed were more concerned with showing themselves to the priests, to get validation of their healing. While only the foreigner felt it more important to come back and praise the God who healed him. I wonder how many times we might be tempted to boast about what God has done for us, rathern than taking time to thank God for the healing we've been given. And how many times we resented that others have been given this gift, especially "foreigners?"

Not all Jesus' healings were curing physical illnesses. Sometimes it was mental illness or spiritual torments that needed to be healed.

> **Matthew 8:28-34 (NIV)** *When he came to the other side into the country of the Gadarenes, two men who were demon-possessed met him as they were coming out of the tombs. They were so extremely violent that no one could pass by that way. And they cried out, saying, "What business do we have with each other, Son of God? Have you come here to torment us before the time?" Now there was a herd of many swine feeding at a distance from them. The demons began to entreat him, saying, "If you are going to cast us out, send us into the herd of swine." And he said to them, "Go!" And they came out and went into the swine, and the whole herd rushed down the steep bank into the sea and perished in the waters. The herdsmen ran away, and went to the city and reported everything, including what had happened to the demoniacs. And behold, the whole city came out to meet Jesus; and when they saw him, they implored him to leave their region.*

Often like the people of Gadarenes, who begged Jesus to leave their region, we may not welcome healing. Sometimes we cling to our illnesses—physical, mental, or spiritual, as a way to remain in our comfortable lives and to ignore God. We really don't want to change; we don't want to be cured. We may not be ready to ask for healing, or to receive it when it is freely

Chapter Four: The Healing Christ

given. We need to face our realities before God can heal them. But Christ is patient with us and will heal us in his time and when we are ready for healing. He will mend our broken bodies, broken souls, broken lives when we are ready.

Chapter Five: The Servant Christ

See this Christ who kneels before you
washing feet of sinful people.

The image of Christ the Servant is one of the most vivid images in the Bible and John relates the story as an eyewitness and as the disciple Jesus loved.

> **John 13:1-17 (NIV)** *It was just before the Passover festival. Jesus knew that the hour had come for him to leave this world and go to the Creator. Having loved his*

See This Christ

own who were in the world, he loved them to the end. The evening meal was in progress, and the devil had already prompted Judas, the son of Simon Iscariot, to betray Jesus. Jesus knew that the Creator had put all things under his power, and that he had come from God and was returning to God; so he got up from the meal, took off his outer clothing, and wrapped a towel around his waist. After that, he poured water into a basin and began to wash his disciples' feet, drying them with the towel that was wrapped around him.

He came to Simon Peter, who said to him, "Lord, are you going to wash my feet?" Jesus replied, "You do not realize now what I am doing, but later you will understand." "No," said Peter, "you shall never wash my feet." Jesus answered, "Unless I wash you, you have no part with me." "Then, Lord," Simon Peter replied, "not just my feet but my hands and my head as well!"

Jesus answered, "Those who have had a bath need only to wash their feet; their whole body is clean. And you are clean, though not every one of you." For he knew who was going to betray him, and that was why he said not everyone was clean.

When he had finished washing their feet, he put on his clothes and returned to his place. "Do you understand what I have done for you?" he asked them. "You call me 'Teacher' and 'Lord,' and rightly so, for that is what I am. Now that I, your Lord and Teacher, have washed your feet, you also should wash one another's feet. I have set

Chapter Five: The Servant Christ

you an example that you should do as I have done for you. Very truly I tell you, no servant is greater than his master, nor is a messenger greater than the one who sent him. Now that you know these things, you will be blessed if you do them.

There is so much richness in this story, it could be a book unto itself. *"Having loved those who were his own in the world, he loved them to the end."* Christ the servant had been with his apostles for three years. He knew their faults and failings. He laughed with them, he cried with them, he taught them, he healed them and helped them heal others, he got angry with them. Sound familiar? It's like any human relationship—we laugh together, we cry together, we know each other's faults, and yet we love each other. But Jesus' love of his disciples was even more challenging than our relationships usually are—his life was coming to an end at the age of thirty-three. He knew one of his friends was about to betray him, which would result in his death. Peter was about to deny he even knew him. James and John had already argued about sitting at his right and left hand when he came into his kingdom. His disciples doubted him at times. They probably thought he spent too much time with sinners—tax collectors, prostitutes, and the like; and questioned his abilities—could he really calm the storm and make Peter walk on the water?

And yet, he loved them to the end!

And now, even though the end was near, they were still questioning him. "What, you are going to wash my feet? Never!" He even tried to explain that although they were "clean," that they were good people and that they would go on to be great people, to do things even greater than he had done, he knew that they were weak, that they still doubted, that just a few short hours later, they wouldn't be able to stay awake and pray with him.

And yet, he loved them to the end.

"Do you understand what I have done for you?" Jesus knew they didn't understand but that after he sent the Holy Spirit, they would understand his overwhelming love for them. Did they understand that he wanted them to go and do for others what he had done for them? Probably not!

And yet, he loved them to the end.

Do we understand what Christ has done for us? Although we didn't literally walk with him on this earth, he gives us the same gifts he gave his disciples. He laughs with us when we are joyous. He weeps with us in our grief. He teaches us though the scriptures and through our interaction with others. He even gets angry with us when we aren't following his teachings. He heals us by giving us his Body and Blood, through listening to his words, and through those we encounter in our lifetime. And yes, he helps us heal others too. He tells all of us we can do even greater things than he did. I find this the most powerful statement in the entire Bible—that he gives us this incredible gift to do great things.

But like his disciples, we doubt him, we deny him, we may even betray his love by getting too caught up in the world, by refusing to love others and ourselves. We question him—can he really do miracles in our lives?

And yet, the Servant Christ loves us to the end.

Chapter Five: The Servant Christ

And, just as he called his apostles to go wash the feet of others, he calls us to do the same.

In my parish, we get to do this quite literally each Holy Thursday when every person in the church gets their feet washed, and every person is invited to wash the feet of others. It's one of the most meaningful expressions of love we can do for each other. But we are called every day to wash the feet of others in so many ways.

Catholic tradition tells us there are seven corporal works of mercy and seven spiritual works of mercy.

Corporal works include feeding the hungry, giving drink to the thirsty, clothing the naked, sheltering the homeless, visiting the sick, visiting the imprisoned, and burying the dead. The spiritual works of mercy include counseling the doubtful, instructing the ignorant, admonishing the sinner, comforting the afflicted, forgiving offenses, bearing wrongs patiently, and praying for the living and the dead. Some of these may come easily, others a little tougher, but we can practice these is our daily lives.

Holding the door for a stranger, letting someone cut in front us in traffic even when we're in a hurry, choking down our road rage and offering instead a nod or a wave of the hand, keeping a child entertained in the grocery line while the frantic parent unloads their cart, being patient with someone who is having a hard day and may be short-tempered with us, calling the lonely widow or widower just to see how he or she is doing, embracing someone who obviously needs a hug, offering a bottle of water to a homeless person on a hot day, welcoming the stranger in our land and helping them adjust, standing up for the persecuted, visiting the prisoner, and yes, forgiving yourself too. This is what the Servant Christ would do, it is what me must do.

Chapter Six: The Dying Christ

See this Christ who hangs here bleeding, weeping, dying for your sins.

See This Christ

We all know the story of Christ's crucifixion. Matthew tells it eloquently.

> **Matthew 27: 33-54 (NIV)** *They came to a place called Golgotha (which means "the place of the skull"). There they offered Jesus wine to drink, mixed with gall; but after tasting it, he refused to drink it. When they had crucified him, they divided up his clothes by casting lots. And sitting down, they kept watch over him there. Above his head they placed the written charge against him: THIS IS JESUS, THE KING OF THE JEWS. Two rebels were crucified with him, one on his right and one on his left. Those who passed by hurled insults at him, shaking their heads and saying, "You who were going to destroy the temple and build it in three days, save yourself! Come down from the cross, if you are the Son of God!" In the same way the chief priests, the teachers of the law and the elders mocked him. "He saved others," they said, "but he can't save himself! He's the king of Israel! Let him come down now from the cross, and we will believe in him. He trusts in God. Let God rescue him now if he wants him, for he said, 'I am the Son of God.'" In the same way the rebels who were crucified with him also heaped insults on him. From noon until three in the afternoon darkness came over all the land. About three in the afternoon Jesus cried out in a loud voice, "Eli, Eli, lemasabachthani?" (which means "My God, my God, why have you forsaken me?"). When some of those standing there heard*

Chapter Six: The Dying Christ

this, they said, "He's calling Elijah." Immediately one of them ran and got a sponge. He filled it with wine vinegar, put it on a staff, and offered it to Jesus to drink. The rest said, "Now leave him alone. Let's see if Elijah comes to save him." And when Jesus had cried out again in a loud voice, he gave up his spirit. At that moment the curtain of the temple was torn in two from top to bottom. The earth shook, the rocks split apart, and the tombs broke open. The bodies of many holy people who had died were raised to life. They came out of the tombs after Jesus' resurrection and went into the holy city and appeared to many people. When the centurion and those with him who were guarding Jesus saw the earthquake and all that had happened, they were terrified, and exclaimed, "Surely he was the Son of God!"

This is Jesus, King of the Jews! Pilate, although much maligned, I have always thought of as an unwitting pawn in the crucifixion story. He tried offering an alternative to crucifixion, he tried to reason with Jesus, and eventually washed his hands of the whole thing. And, when questioned about the sign above Jesus' head and told he should have written, "This man *said* he was king of the Jews," he answered, "what I have written, I have written." A fitting epitaph for the King.

I wonder what people thought when they saw that sign? It sems like crucifixions drew big crowds. And this one probably more than usual. The Pharisees and high priests were there, maybe to make sure he didn't somehow come down from the cross, and were gloating when it became obvious this man was

See This Christ

going to die, just like every other "criminal" that was hung on a cross to suffocate. The average onlooker was there, perhaps out of morbid curiosity, perhaps because they were hoping to witness another miracle. Most of his disciples were not there, out of fear! Only John stood with the women at the cross.

So much of humanity is reflected through the witnesses to the crucifixion. How many of us ignore the signs that clearly point to Jesus as King? While we might not see a physical sign "This is Jesus, the King of the Jews," we are given many signs if we are open to seeing them, and hearing them, and touching them. Are we open to full meaning of the scriptures when we hear them or read them? Do we really understand that we see Jesus in every person we meet, even the people we don't like, the people who are different from us, the people who may not even believe in Jesus? But he is there. Do we feel Jesus when we touch a dying person's hand, when we reach out to lift someone who has fallen, when we make love?

How many times do we, like some of the witnesses to the crucifixion, gloat over other people's misfortune? He deserved that! She had it coming to her! Boy, I'm glad I didn't listen to him. I knew she was bad, and this just proves it!

And how many times do we, like the disciples, just avoid conflict altogether. I am afraid if I speak my mind, people will think less of me. I don't want to be seen anywhere near that person, or people will think I am like that. I will look the other way when I see the homeless on the street. I will assume that "hooker" standing on the corner is there because she is a sinner, not because she may be a victim of human trafficking. I will condemn the rich because they must be evil people. I will look the other way when injustices are right in front of me.

Chapter Six: The Dying Christ

Jesus died and wept not for himself, but for our sins. Let's at least show him the courtesy of drying his tears, of wiping the blood. A very wise woman who attended a retreat with me said "you can't embrace the cross without getting blood on your hands."

"How," you might be saying, "can I wipe Jesus' blood and tears away?" If only I would have been there, I would have done it. "If only." Two of the most dangerous words in the English language. If only I had time to help my neighbor who needs a ride to the store. If only that person didn't treat me so poorly, I could find it in my heart to love them. If only my family obligations weren't so demanding, I could find time to help at church. If only I wasn't so busy at work, I could spend more time with my kids. If only I was smarter, younger, thinner, less afraid, I could do……. The "if onlys" seem to go on and on, don't they? You can wipe away Jesus' blood and tears, if only you see them and care enough to do something about it. You can do it every day. When you meet Jesus around you. In your family, in your friends, in your neighbor (that is everybody of course.)

As we read above, Matthew tells us:

About three in the afternoon Jesus cried out in a loud voice, "Eli, Eli, lemasabachthani?" (which means "My God, my God, why have you forsaken me?").

How many times have felt forsaken by God? Probably more than once for most of us. Even Jesus cried and felt deserted by his friends and even his God. So, maybe when you are feeling that way, this might be a good time to reflect on this verse. And know that even if your friends forsake you, God has not.

See This Christ

There are things God has in store for you that you might not understand during these lonely, grief-filled times, but you will see them later.

> *And when Jesus had cried out again in a loud voice, he gave up his spirit. At that moment the curtain of the temple was torn in two from top to bottom. The earth shook, the rocks split apart, and the tombs broke open.... When the centurion and those with him who were guarding Jesus saw the earthquake and all that had happened, they were terrified, and exclaimed, "Surely he was the Son of God!"*

Again, we see the Roman centurions accepting Christ as the Son of God. The foreigner. The ones who occupied the land of the Jews. The hated ones. The powerful ones. Jesus revealed himself to a pretty motley crew of people when you think about it. Tax collectors, Romans, Samaritans, women, prostitutes, Pharisees, fisherman, traitors, thieves, insurrectionists, lepers, all were touched by this Christ during his life and as he hung on the cross, bleeding, weeping, dying for all of them, and for all of us—the powerful, the rich, the poor, the blind, the homeless, the helpless, the believer, the nonbeliever, those of every nationality, every color, every religion. Just so we would learn to wash the blood and tears of each other.

Chapter Seven: The Risen Christ

*See this Christ in all His glory,
risen now triumphantly.*

All the images of Christ we've discussed so far, come together in the risen Christ—the joyful, the sad, the healing, the suffering, the angry, and the teaching Christ. The destiny of Christ, and of us, is resurrection.

> **John 20:1-18 (NAS)** *Now on the first day of the week Mary Magdalene came early to the tomb, while it was still dark, and saw the stone already taken away from*

See This Christ

the tomb. So, she ran and came to Simon Peter and to the other disciple whom Jesus loved, and said to them, "They have taken away the Lord out of the tomb, and we do not know where they have laid him." So, Peter and the other disciple went forth, and they were going to the tomb. The two were running together; and the other disciple ran ahead faster than Peter and came to the tomb first; and stooping and looking in, he saw the linen wrappings lying there; but he did not go in. And so Simon Peter also came, following him, and entered the tomb; and he saw the linen wrappings lying there, and the face-cloth which had been on his head, not lying with the linen wrappings, but rolled up in a place by itself. So, the other disciple who had first come to the tomb then also entered, and he saw and believed. For they did not yet understand the scripture, that he must rise again from the dead. So, the disciples went away again to their own homes.

But Mary was standing outside the tomb weeping; and so, as she wept, she stooped and looked into the tomb; and she saw two angels in white sitting, one at the head and one at the feet, where the body of Jesus had been lying. And they said to her, "Woman, why are you weeping?" She said to them, "Because they have taken away my Lord, and I do not know where they have laid him." When she had said this, she turned around and saw Jesus standing there, and did not know that it was Jesus. Jesus said to her, "Woman, why are you weeping? Whom are you seeking" Supposing him to be the gardener, she said to him, "Sir, if you have carried him away, tell me where you have laid him, and I will take him away."

Chapter Seven: The Risen Christ

Jesus said to her, "Mary!" She turned and said to Him in Hebrew, "Rabboni!" (which means, Teacher). Jesus said to her, "Stop clinging to me, for I have not yet ascended to the Creator; but go to my brothers and say to them, 'I ascend to my Creator and your Creator, and my God and your God.'" Mary Magdalene came, announcing to the disciples, "I have seen the Lord," and that he had said these things to her.

In this scripture passage we see all of salvation, and all humanity's doubts, fears, and ultimately belief, laid out clearly for us. Mary's faith that somehow when she got to the tomb, there would be someone to help her roll away that heavy stone in the first incredible part of this story. Some might think, "Well, she shouldn't have gone there without a plan." Foolish woman. I know I would have said that. I don't do well without a plan in place for everything in my life. But God often laughs at our plans and has a totally different plan in mind for us. Although scripture doesn't tell us Mary entered the tomb, I believe that her curiosity would have taken over and she would have looked around for Jesus's body. After all, she carried those oils a long way, didn't she? You would think she'd want to know exactly why the stone was rolled away and who did it. Was it possible the person who did this was still hanging around somewhere?

But, in her eagerness to share this astounding news she hightailed it back to where the apostles were hiding to tell them what had happened.

Peter and John often seem to be at odds with each other during their time with Jesus and there was certainly some competition among the disciples. John, perhaps because he was younger, won this race. Why did he not enter the tomb? Like Mary, perhaps he was afraid of what he would find. Perhaps grave robbers broke in and mutilated Christ's body. Perhaps they had indeed removed his body and his followers would never find it. Peter, always a bit impetuous, enters boldly. That's his style although he often backs off when he realizes what he's done. Like he did when Jesus called him to walk on water, he jumped right in, but then his faith wavered. He was probably feeling a bit tremulous now. "I entered this tomb to see what is going on, but now I'm more perplexed than ever!"

But the clue to what happened was in the folded face cloth. Surely someone had deliberately folded it and set it aside from the other burial garments. I've been told that the folded cloth was symbolic of the master who folds his napkin at dinner; he does so to let the servants know he is planning to return to the table. Although Peter, John, and Mary may not yet have fully understood the implications of the empty tomb, they knew something very unusual had happened. Peter and John returned home, perhaps to ponder this event, to pray, to discuss with the other apostles what all this meant. It took them some time to realize that Jesus was returning, had indeed already returned.

But Mary remained. And she was rewarded when she encounters someone that could at last provide some hope, some answers. Maybe the "gardener" knew what had happened.

"Mary." Just one word! All it took was for Jesus to call her name. And she suddenly knew what had happened! It was indeed the risen Christ. "Rabboni, teacher" it is really you.

Perhaps like me, you've wondered why Jesus told Mary not

Chapter Seven: The Risen Christ

to embrace him. Surely, he had great affection for Mary, and she for him. Wouldn't it be natural for two friends to embrace at a moment like this? It has always puzzled me. But I think I am beginning to understand it better.

One of my favorite quotes from Kahlil Gibran in *The Prophet* has helped me understand this distancing Jesus imposed on Mary during this encounter:

> *Let there be spaces in your togetherness and let the winds of the heavens dance between you. Love one another but make not a bond of love: Let it rather be a moving sea between the shores of your souls. Fill each other's cup but drink not from one cup. Give one another of your bread but eat not from the same loaf. Sing and dance together and be joyous, but let each one of you be alone, even as the strings of a lute are alone though they quiver with the same music. Give your hearts, but not into each other's keeping. For only the hand of Life can contain your hearts. And stand together, yet not too near together: For the pillars of the temple stand apart, And the oak tree and the cypress grow not in each other's shadow.*

This passage from Gibran has always been a great reminder to husbands and wives, but also to friends. That we each must be our own person, to stand firm in our own faith and not to be dependent on any other human being. Of course, we need to be dependent on Jesus, but we must rely on ourselves at times. I am beginning to see that what Jesus may have been saying to Mary is "you are to be a great apostle, but I will not be with

See This Christ

you in body very long so don't get too "clingy" as we would say today. Don't depend on me to solve all your issues and protect you from the trials of this world. Rise, get up and go about your business, just as he told those he healed. Be my disciple, speak up for justice in the world, tell others what you have witnessed, help other to know me as you have known me. The Risen Christ asks us all to do what he was telling Mary. Don't just delight in my resurrection and keep it to yourself. Go tell the others what you have seen!

Like Peter and John, we may be in competition with people of other faiths, or even our own faith, to find and tell the "real story." We may want to be holier than our brothers and sisters. We may want to feel especially blessed by our Lord. We may want to have the kind of faith we see in others. Stop! It's not a contest! Someone else's blessing, someone ese's faith, someone else's holiness, someone else's knowledge does not diminish our own. Maybe our blessings take a different form, maybe we are knowledgeable in different areas, maybe our faith is just as strong if we allow it to flourish. We cannot walk someone's journey; we walk our own. And it doesn't matter who gets to the empty tomb first! We each get there in our time, in our own way.

Like Mary Magdalen, when we do encounter Jesus in or lives, we may want to enjoy this peace within or own hearts. To enjoy being alone with Jesus and be embraced by him. But his arms are always around us when we go out of our comfort zone, when we take that leap of faith. So, be joyful at the Lord's resurrection. But don't try to contain that joy within yourself, share it.

Chapter Eight: The Loving Christ

See this Christ who loves you,
and wants you to be with him every day.
Yes, he wants you to be with him in all ways.
Every day.

Of all the sides of Christ we've seen so far, perhaps the most important for us, is the Loving Christ. And yet, sometimes it is most difficult face of Christ for us to recognize and to understand.

> **Romans 8: 35, 37-39 (NAS)** *Who will separate us from the love of Christ? Will tribulation, or distress, or*

See This Christ

persecution, or famine, or nakedness, or peril, or sword? ......But in all these things we overwhelmingly conquer through him who loved us. For I am convinced that neither death, nor life, nor angels, nor principalities, nor things present, nor things to come, nor powers, nor height, nor depth, nor any other created thing, will be able to separate us from the love of God, which is in Christ Jesus our Lord.

First, we need to understand the meaning of love. Our English language is lacking in many ways, because we only have one word to describe the many nuances of a thing like love. There are several Greek words for love, and to truly understand Jesus's love we need to understand the nuances of the word love as it was used in scriptures. You don't need to be a Biblical scholar or study Greek and Aramaic to understand the Bible, but it helps if you understand the subtleties of these languages in order to better understand scripture. So, indulge me while I present a description of the various types of love used in scriptures.

- ◆ *Agape:* means "the love of God for humans and of humans for a good God." Agape is used by Christians to express the unconditional love of God for all people. Agape is used in ancient texts to denote a God-like love, and it was also used to refer to a love feast, which is celebrated by Christian faiths such as the Moravians, who even have a special Moravian Sugar Cakes, a pastry which is used during the love feast. Catholics and other Christians also celebrated an

Chapter Eight: The Loving Christ

Agape feast as a para-liturgical celebration after mass, often during the Easter Triduum.

- *Eros* means "love, mostly of the sexual passion". The Modern Greek word "erotas" means "intimate love." Plato says that although eros is initially felt for a person, with contemplation it becomes an appreciation of the beauty within that person, or even becomes appreciation of beauty itself. Socrates argued that eros helps the soul recall knowledge of beauty, and contributes to an understanding of spiritual truth, the ideal form of youthful beauty that leads us humans to feel erotic desire – thus suggesting that even that sensually based love aspires to the non-corporeal, spiritual plane of existence; that is, finding its truth, just like finding any truth, leads to transcendence.

- *Philia* means "affectionate regard, friendship", usually "between equals." It is a dispassionate virtuous love, a concept developed by Aristotle. Philia is expressed variously as loyalty to friends (specifically, "brotherly love"), family, and community, and requires virtue, equality, and familiarity.

- *Storge* means "love, affection" especially of parents and children. It is the common or natural empathy, like that felt by parents for offspring. In ancient works, it almost exclusively describes relationships within the family. It is also used when referencing the love for one's country or a favorite sports team.

See This Christ

- *Philautia* means "self-love" to love yourself or "regard for one's own happiness or advantage" has both been conceptualized as a basic human necessity or as a moral flaw, akin to vanity and selfishness. The Greeks further divided this love into positive and negative: one the unhealthy version is the self-obsessed love, and the other is the concept of "self-compassion."
- *Xenia* meaning "guest-friendship," is the ancient Greek concept of hospitality, the generosity and courtesy shown to those who are far from home. The rituals of hospitality created and expressed a reciprocal relationship between guest and host expressed in both material benefits (such as the giving of gifts to each party) as well as non-material ones (such as protection, shelter, favors, or certain human rights).

One of the best ways to understand the loving Christ is to reflect on John 21:15-17. Jesus, soon after his resurrection, spotted his apostles fishing and decided to cook them breakfast. After their shared meal, Jesus asked Peter three times, "Do you love me?" Jesus used this opportunity to encourage and exhort Peter about his upcoming responsibilities. By asking Peter, "Do you love me?" three times, Jesus was emphasizing the importance of Peter's love and his faith that would be necessary for his future ministry.

Jesus begins by questioning Peter about his love for him, and each time Peter answers in the affirmative, Jesus follows up with the command for Peter to feed his sheep. His meaning is that, if Peter truly loves him, he will be required to shepherd and care for those who belong to Christ.

Chapter Eight: The Loving Christ

The full meaning of this discourse is not clear until you look at the Greek words for "love" used in this exchange between Jesus and Peter. When Jesus asked Peter, "Do you love me?" the first two times he used the Greek word *agape*, which refers to unconditional love. Both times, Peter responded with "Yes, Lord; you know that I love you," using the Greek word, *philia*, which refers more to a brotherly/friendship love. It seems that Jesus is trying to get Peter to understand that he must love Jesus unconditionally in order to be the leader God is calling him to be. The third time Jesus asks, "Do you love me?" Jesus himself uses the word *philia*, and Peter again responds with "Lord, you know everything; you know that I love you," again using *philia*. The point is that by using the different Greek words for "love" Jesus was stretching Peter to move him from *philia* love to *agape* love.

Jesus wanted Peter, and he wants us, to love with that unconditional, *agape* love with which he loved us. Throughout scripture there are many instances of Jesus loving those who perhaps didn't deserve his love, but he gave it freely anyway. And he loves us with the same unconditional love, which seems to encompass all the other forms of love. He wants us to love him the same way, even when we may be disappointed because we feel he hasn't heard our prayers, or perhaps because he showers that unconditional love on people we don't think are deserving of his love.

And, he wants us to give that same unconditional love to everyone. Now, that's a tall order to fill. It is easy to love with agape love if you already have some of the other kinds love in your heart. The *eros* love between husband and wife makes it easier to forgive faults, the *philia* love we feel towards our friends makes it easier to overlook their failings. The *storge* love and affection we feel towards our children make it easier to love them even when they disappoint us or break off relations with us.

These kinds of loves make *agape* love easier. If we have a strong relationship with someone, it is easier to feel that unconditional *agape* love.

Perhaps the two kinds of love that most of us struggle with are *philautia* (self-love) and *xenia*, the hospitality to strangers.

Self-love challenges us to draw the line between narcissism and the love Jesus refers to when he tells us about the two greatest commandments—to love God with all our heart, all our soul, all our mind, and all our strength; and to love or neighbor *as* ourselves. Not love your neighbor *more* than you love yourself, or *less* than you love yourself, but *as* you love yourself. On an equal level. Self-love is required before we can love others. If we have no respect for ourselves, we cannot respect others.

Xenia, or hospitality, is the other form of love that many of us struggle with. It is easy to love friends, relatives, and maybe even ourselves, because we know these people. But to show hospitality to the stranger goes beyond loving those who love us and are known to us. It may also be why we find it sometimes hard, like Peter did, to love Christ with that unconditional *agape* love. We need to *know* Jesus in order to love him.

To Know Him Is to Love Him, To Love Him is to Know Him

Years ago, there was a popular song, "To Know Him Is to Love Him" written by Phil Spector, inspired by words on his father's tombstone, "To Know Him Was To Love Him." It was

Chapter Eight: The Loving Christ

first recorded by the Teddy Bears, and later by Dolly Parton, Linda Ronstadt, and Emmylou Harris, in their album, *Trio*, among others.

As with the word love, "know" has several meanings in ancient Greek.

It can mean "to understand, to make apparent, to proclaim, to be visible." It is from the Greek word, *gnostos*. You may be familiar with the term Gnostics, a group that emphasized personal spiritual knowledge (*gnosis*) over orthodox teachings, traditions, and ecclesiastical authority. They considered the principal element of salvation to be direct knowledge of the supreme divinity. Gnosticism presents a distinction between a supreme, transcendent God and a blind, evil spirit responsible for creating the material universe. Many Gnostic texts deal not in concepts of sin and repentance, but with illusion and enlightenment. If this term is not familiar to you, you are surely familiar with the word, agnostic—those who do not know.

The Greek word *epignosis* denotes "exact or full knowledge, discernment, recognition, expressing a fuller or a full knowledge, a greater participation by the knower in the object known, acknowledging the truth, the mystery of God.

The word, know, is used by scripture writers is different ways. For example, when Mary tells Gabriel, she cannot possibly be pregnant because she does not "know man." She is referring to an intimacy of knowing in a sexual way. But intimacy isn't always sexual.

Knowing God implies having an intimacy with God, not only an intellectual understanding. Richard Rohr says that we

See This Christ

come to know God by loving God and that love is the highest form of knowledge. Saint John of the Cross and many mystics and theologians agree with Rohr. Saint Augustine said, "Love is the highest form of knowing." Loving and knowing are sort of a "chicken and egg" mystery. Do you have to know God in order to love God? Do you have to love God in order to know God? We can never know God in a physical way. As Rohr says, "God is incomprehensible to the intellect." And John of the Cross says, "God can be loved, but not thought." So, to know God is to love God, but to love God is also to know God.

Loving and knowing God is really feeling Christ present in your life and being willing to share that unconditional agape love with Christ and with everyone—family, friends, strangers. Jesus made this clear to his apostles.

> **John 15:13-17 (NAS)** *This is my commandment, that you love one another, just as I have loved you. "Greater love has no one than this, that one lay down his life for his friends. You are my friends if you do what I command you. No longer do I call you slaves, for the slave does not know what his master is doing; but I have called you friends, for all things that I have heard from my Creator I have made known to you. You did not choose me but I chose you, and appointed you that you would go and bear fruit, and that your fruit would remain, so that whatever you ask of the Creator in my name the Creator may give to you. This I command you, that you love one another.*

He calls us, along with the apostles, to be his friends, his beloved, and to share his *agape* love with others.

Chapter Eight: The Loving Christ

Ephesians 5:1-2 (NAS) *Therefore be imitators of God, as beloved children; and walk in love, just as Christ also loved you and gave himself up for us, an offering and a sacrifice to God as a fragrant aroma.*

St Paul, in his letter to the Ephesians, likewise, reminds us of the fact that we are loved by Christ and that his sacrifice should be treated as a "fragrant aroma," a sweet and joy-filled experience. We are an Easter people. Let's act like it!

I John 2: 7-10 (NAS) *Beloved, I am not writing a new commandment to you, but an old commandment which you have had from the beginning; the old commandment is the word which you have heard. On the other hand, I am writing a new commandment to you, which is true in him and in you, because the darkness is passing away and the true light is already shining. The one who says he is in the light and yet hates his brother is in the darkness until now. The one who loves his brother abides in the light and there is no cause for stumbling in him.*

John, the disciple Jesus loved, reminds us of the "both/and" concept. This is not a new commandment, it existed before the beginning of time, and yet it is new because Jesus showed us what walking in the light really means. We are to be the light for the world, we are not to hide our light under a basket, but let it shine on a hill for all to see.

1 Peter 4:8-11 (NAS) *Above all, keep fervent in your love for one another, because love covers a multitude of sins. Be hospitable to one another without complaint. As each one*

See This Christ

> *has received a special gift, employ it in serving one another as good stewards of the manifold grace of God. Whoever speaks, is to do so as one who is speaking the utterances of God; whoever serves is to do so as one who is serving by the strength which God supplies; so that in all things God may be glorified through Jesus Christ, to whom belongs the glory and dominion forever and ever. Amen.*

Although Peter seemed reluctant to express the *agape* love that Christ asked him to affirm, he certainly seemed to have a good grasp on what Jesus was asking of him, and us, when he wrote this passage. We are called to use our special talents and abilities to serve God, and to serve others. To love God, and to love others. This is what Jesus calls us to do, to accept his love, and to love him, ourselves, and our neighbors with true *agape* love.

The amazing thing about Christ's agape love is that we are all called to be the Body of Christ. When we receive the Body of Christ, we become that Body for others and if we truly See This Christ, we become one with him. So how do we become Christ's Body?

The Laughing Christ—we must find joy in our lives and instill joy in all we meet—we must learn to dance in the streets with the children (and the young adults, the middle-aged, and the elderly) Laugh as Jesus laughed. Laugh at yourself and laugh with others.

The Teaching Christ—while you may not think of yourself as a teacher, you are! You may not always be required to instruct with words, but your actions are teaching actions. As Saint Francis said, "Preach always and, if you must, use words." Be a storyteller but tell Jesus' story with your words and your actions.

Chapter Eight: The Loving Christ

The Angry Christ—yes, feel free to express anger at injustice. We often hear people say, "I'm not political. I prefer to mind my own business. I can't get upset about what is going on in the world." But consider the root of the word political (of the people). It's about people, about God's creation. If you see injustice, *make* it your business. And don't be afraid to get angry and upset when you see inequality in the world. Jesus got angry, and we should also realize there is a time for just anger.

The Healing Christ—again you might feel you are not a healer, but you don't have to be a doctor, a nurse, a shaman, or a saint to heal. Use healing words, reach out and touch someone when they need a hug, offer a kind word to someone who is having a bad day, pray for someone who is sick in mind, body, or spirit. You may not realize it, but you can bring healing to others, physically, mentally, or spiritually.

The Servant Christ—we hear a lot about servant leadership, the concept of leading by empowering others. We have so many opportunities to wash each other's feet, metaphorically, if not literally. This doesn't mean being subservient to, or allowing yourself to be treated badly by, anyone. It means showing others that their well-being is important to you. True servant leadership is empowering for the server and the served.

The Dying Christ—of course, we are all dying from the moment we're born, but we are called to die to the world while we live in it. This doesn't mean retreating from the world. It means using our sufferings to understand that this suffering can be redemptive for us and others. It is good for us to contemplate Christ's bleeding, dying body from time to time, not just on Good Friday, and to understand to what in our life is he asking us to die.

See This Christ

The Risen Christ—we all have the hope of eternal life with Christ. But do we act like an Easter People? Do we really believe that we should be joyful Christians, focused on the risen Christ in all his glory, knowing that we too are glorious, wonderful creatures created in God's image? If we believe that, let's act like it!

The Loving Christ—we are, above all, called to love our neighbor as ourselves. We show this love by laughing, by teaching, yes, even by being angry at injustice. We show it by healing and being willing to be healed. We show it by being servants and by allowing ourselves to be served. We show it by dying and by rising.

I close this reflection with a quote from one of my personal heroes, with whom I am proud to share her birthday (although not the same year), Dorothy Day, founder of the Catholic Worker movement and author of a number of books, including *The Reckless Way of Love: Notes on Following Jesus First*.

> *I really only love God as much as I love the person I love the least.*

—*Dorothy Day*